Don't Tell the Children

Empowering Society to Talk Openly About Death, Grief and Funerals

John Adams

with Clare Shaw

First published in Great Britain in 2024

by Clare Shaw Children's Books

PO12 2PN

www.cskidsbooks.com

ISBN 978-0-9957596-8-8

Memento Mori

"Remember you must die"

Contents

Introduction

Have you ever had to arrange a funeral? Or look after a bereaved child? People don't know where to start. It can be very easy to feel lost when living through grief. This book has been carefully put together to offer support when this happens to you, whether you're in the midst of it now or when it happens in the future.

Having both experienced grief at a very young age we, John Adams and Clare Shaw, are now working together to help children and families experiencing the same thing. John, a 4th generation funeral director, and Clare, an author of mental wellbeing books for children and teens, give our own stories of loss, along with practical and emotional guidance.

We want to empower future generations to discuss death, dying and bereavement more openly. Thus, making these painful moments more manageable. We will give some insight into how children might deal with death at certain developmental stages and, in addition, offer practical tips that are proven to really help.

John has compiled a step-by-step guide as to what to do when someone dies. Who do you call? What choices do you have? John will cover this in detail, including some "Frequently Asked Questions" that he has come across within his line of work.

We offer a section for schools and professionals working with children. Our hope and vision for the future is one where children - and adults - feel comfortable discussing death in a healthy open manner.

While writing this book, we reached out to the wider public to ask for their experience of arranging a funeral and what they wished they'd known before the event. Their responses were so powerful that we've added them exactly as they were sent to us in the hope that their lived experiences can help you in the future.

We will talk a lot about the children, but this book is just as much about the adults reading it. This book can help everyone.

Part 1

Child Bereavement: Coping with Grief as a Family

John's Story

My name is John Adams, 4th generation funeral director, National Association of Funeral Directors (NAFD) approved tutor and Funeral Industry Advisor to Child Bereavement UK. At the age of twelve my mum, Maria, died, which had a profound impact on my life. At the age of 18, I joined the Royal Navy and served for eight years, finishing my time as an Electronic Warfare Director classified to top secret. I re-joined my family funeral service, Perry & Phillips in 2012, a decade on I was elected to become National President of the NAFD, which is the largest funeral trade association in the UK. During this time, I launched a parliamentary petition to add content on death, dying and bereavement into the national curriculum, nearly 12,000 signatures were obtained and Government responded that a public consultation would be carried out by the Department for Education, acknowledging the importance of bereavement awareness being taught. I have had the privilege of speaking on stages all over the UK to discuss this important initiative, funeral industry related matters and my views on life and death. My ultimate goal in life is to "inspire society and help our future, dedicating myself to highlight the path of resilience and positivity, even in the darkest of moments, driving for a stronger, brighter environment for all".

Whilst working on this book, and carrying out my mission to add content on death and bereavement into classrooms, it has made me think back, connect and reflect on my own experience at school and surroundings when my mum died. The overriding feeling is that it was a lonely time, however, I do not feel sorry for the twelve year old John, the experience has given me a clear vision on how we can make the experience of loss better for all of society. A child loses a parent every 20 minutes in the UK, this eye opening statistic does not include the loss of siblings, aunties, uncles, grandparents and even pets. I joined secondary school with my mum critically ill, at that time I was constantly worried and concerned for her health, my dad had always been very honest that she would die from this illness, this was the harsh reality but it also ensured I had no regrets when my mum eventually died. Everything I needed to say was said, every hug meant more, despite being twelve years of age I was aware she was at some point going to leave us. My dad 'told the children' - I am grateful and proud that he did that.

The time prior to my mum's death was also my first insight into separation. My mum was a very determined individual and with this fighting attitude she explored alternative medicines to prolong her life, one of which was to spend over six months in a cancer retreat centre in Poland trying treatments that were not available or even heard of in the UK. These methods and alternative medicines did provide her more time with her family, I admire the determination she showed in trying to survive. After initially been given twelve months to live from her first diagnosis; with her fight, she went on to live for six years longer than the original prognosis. Despite her time spent away finding ways to live longer, which for a twelve year old was a very difficult pill to swallow, the love I received from my mum was extraordinary. I often say now when giving talks on stages, I feel so grateful to have had my mum for those initial twelve years of my life. She has given me true foundations for a lifetime, what a woman and what a mum.

Due to these challenges, at school I never really felt like I fitted in. The school missed wonderful opportunities to create connections which would have been positive for all. An example being that the head of my year still had no awareness that my mum had died three to four months after her death, despite my dad writing to the school on her initial passing. On reflection, what a missed opportunity for better communication channels and to share why we need to get behind each other when times get tough. Even if unsure what to say, simply asking someone if they are ok can really start healthy steps forward in a supportive community.

Throughout mum's illness and death, my sister Katie dealt with it differently to me. She was fourteen years old and became a lone wolf, appearing strong and not needing any help. She was remarkable in the care and support she provided her, even shaving mum's head after her chemotherapy treatment.

My dad's reaction to his wife's death was to get on with it. Due to the high demands of running a funeral directors he very much wanted to move forward with his life and get on with things following six years of desperation and battling. His 'getting on with it' also meant bringing up two young children which I know would have been a huge challenge for any widowed parent.

Maria sadly died on July 14th 1998. She made the decision to spend her final few weeks at her mother's home. This was to try and protect my sister and me from the memories of her dying at our family home. Despite this being a very sad moment, it was also a very poignant time. Looking back, I am very proud I was able to reassure her, whispering in her ear "I promise we will all be fine, and now it was her time to go".

I was exposed to the closest level of loss at the age of twelve. At a young age your world is pretty small. The facts are though, we are all touched by death, loss or a tragedy at some point in our lives. The country was grieving when we experienced the death of Queen Elizabeth II in 2022. Throughout the Covid pandemic we saw the number of deaths every day on various media channels. Death is all around us, we cannot avoid it and it is the only guaranteed event in all our lives! It is my belief that when we have a basic understanding of death and the vast range of emotions that can be associated with it, it is then when we can start living our true lives and appreciate the small things. Why wait until we get the devasting diagnosis before we start completing our bucket list and be grateful of our surroundings? Not only will open dialogue help the child that loses a family member, but teaching children who have not yet suffered a loss will also enable them to have some understanding and compassion for others who may be experiencing it. These young people will grow into adults who should be able to have more open conversations with their peers who have suffered a loss, instead of crossing the road to avoid an uncomfortable conversation.

Using my experience, including arranging funerals and delivering training for funeral professionals, I believe in empowering the bereaved, ensuring that they understand they have choices. With true empowerment the bereaved can begin their grief journey in a more positive position, and with specific and more personalised connection points, which we will cover throughout this book, every grief journey can be in a stronger place for the now and for the future.

When starting the parliamentary petition, in October 2022, to add content on death, dying and bereavement to the national curriculum as a compulsory session, I did not foresee how all these areas that mean so much to me are all connected. The unknown creates fear, educate about the unknown and you will reduce the fear. Education and awareness is working in a proactive manner rather than knee jerk guessing in the dark.

This book is a tool for all of society, from young to old, to those that agree with my philosophy and those who believe we still need to keep children away from these important discussions. I hope by the end of this book you will feel that by using honest, age-appropriate education, spoken with love, kindness and bravery, we have the opportunity to help society be more empathetic of what people might be going through. Simple methods of communication or acts of kindness can have a profound impact on your environment. The potential of this kinder society is a place and environment I would like my children to grow up in and one I believe we should all be striving towards.

Let's empower young people, teaching them about the emotions associated with loss and separation, lets teach them about patience, compassion and kindness.

It's time to tell the children.

Empowering Future Generations with Grief and Loss

Grief and loss are a natural part of life; therefore, empowering future generations with the knowledge and tools to navigate these difficult experiences seems an obvious thing to do. So, why do so many people avoid the conversation?

In our culture it has long been a taboo subject. Death is a topic that can feel uncomfortable and challenging to talk about, even more so when those conversations involve children. However, avoiding these conversations can do more harm than good. Avoidance can leave children feeling confused, isolated, and ill-equipped to cope with the inevitable losses they will encounter throughout their lives. When we initiate discussions about death and grief, we provide children with a foundation of understanding that can help them when they lose a loved one themselves, as a child or even into adulthood.

Many children, teens and even some adults, only really learn about death when the inevitable happens to a loved one of theirs. Uncomfortable as it may be, talking openly about death allows children to develop a realistic perspective on mortality. It helps them grasp the concept of death as a natural part of life's cycle and reduces the fear and anxiety often associated with it. By acknowledging death as "normal", we empower children to develop healthy coping mechanisms and a positive attitude towards life, even emphasising the importance of cherishing each moment and nurturing meaningful connections with others.

By engaging in age-appropriate conversations about death before it is experienced, we create an environment where children feel safe to express their thoughts, feelings, and questions. Family, caregivers, educators, and support professionals play a crucial role in facilitating these conversations and providing the necessary support. It is important to approach these discussions with empathy, patience, and sensitivity, allowing children to express themselves without judgment or fear. This can help children to develop resilience, emotional intelligence, and a genuine understanding of loss. It allows the adults to recognise and address children's unique emotional needs. As well as their own.

Whether a child has already lost someone they love or not, a great way to create a safe space for open dialogue is by actively listening to children's experiences and validating their emotions. For those who have lost, doing this shows them that it is normal and acceptable to experience grief and that they are not alone in their struggles. Encouraging children to share their thoughts and questions, even if they seem difficult or uncomfortable, promotes a sense of trust and openness. This can be done through regular check-ins, one-on-one conversations, or group discussions where children can share their experiences and learn from one another. (The latter can be achieved through a school setting or local bereavement group.)

It is important to recognise that children experience and process grief differently than adults. Their understanding of death evolves as they grow, and their emotional needs vary based on their developmental stage. By acknowledging and addressing these differences, we can provide age-appropriate support that meets their specific needs, both at home and within a professional environment.

Remember, discussing death and grief with children is not about overwhelming them with darkness, but rather about providing them with the tools to find light, strength, and healing in the face of loss. The more we normalise these conversations, the easier we, and future generations, will find them.

Age Related Understanding

A child's response to death can depend on a number of factors; their age, their relationship with the deceased and the family's belief system, as examples. How children deal with their grief will be dependent on the support they have around them - which can be tricky when the rest of the family are also grieving.

Under Five

Younger children may struggle with abstract concepts like permanence and separation. They may have difficulty understanding that death is itself final and irreversible. Up to around the age of four there is little understanding from the child as to what has happened. They will sense that something is different and that those around them are sad. As difficult as it can be, it is best to try to stick to a routine. Try to keep things as normal as possible for them to give them a sense of security. If they are old enough to ask questions, always answer honestly. Using phrases such as "Granny's gone to sleep" can be extremely damaging to young children. This could create a fear of falling asleep, or seeing others do so.

Explaining death as the end of living or as "not being able to come back" can provide a starting point for their understanding. Reassuring them that death is a natural part of life, using simple yet straightforward language, can help them navigate their grief.

Five to Eight Years

Once children reach between five and eight they start to understand the finality of death. Similarly to addressing younger children, this age group will benefit from honesty and direct language. They may ask a lot of questions, and repeat these questions until they cement their understanding. The more open and honest those around them are at this point, the easier it will be for them to reconcile and understand. Trying to find ways to make things 'easier' for them by using euphemisms could actually make things much harder for them in the future.

At this age children have also developed 'Magical Thinking'. They believe that their thoughts and wishes can absolutely come true! This can lead them to believe that something they said or did caused their loved one's death. Listen to their concerns and offer reassurance. Try to avoid phrases such as "don't be silly", if they believe you think their questions are silly, they may stop asking or even talking about how they feel at all. They may need some encouragement to express their emotions. It may be too difficult to verbalise so drawing, writing and play can help with this. Reassurance is key.

Nine to Twelve Years

As children enter their pre-teens, their understanding of death becomes more nuanced. Between the ages of 9 and 12 they may look more closely at those around them to work out how they should be behaving. Try to be as open as possible about your own feelings to encourage and support their need to express themselves. If this is their first funeral, they may be concerned about what they might see. They may have lots of questions that they deem to be 'ridiculous' eg "Will I see the body?", "What will I wear?". Try to explain as much as possible; whether they ask the questions or not! If the family don't know, the funeral arranger will be able to help with this.

They may have 'musings' about the afterlife, the meaning of life and death, and the impact of death on their own mortality. Engaging in open discussions about these topics, acknowledging their curiosity, and encouraging their exploration can promote their emotional growth and resilience. By providing them with accurate information and addressing their enquiries, we can help them develop a healthy perspective on death.

Teenagers

When children hit their teens, they are going through so many social, emotional and hormonal changes anyway, adding grief to the mix can be quite tricky. They may cover up their emotions to protect those around them. They may also cover them to appear strong and put on a brave face. Depending on who has died, they may feel they have to look after other family members and be 'responsible'.

It's possible they'll want to be around friends more so than family but may not talk to those friends about how they're feeling. Keep checking in. Find the right way to do so that supports the individual.

Autistic Children

As with all children, autistic children and those with learning difficulties, need their feelings to be acknowledged and understood. Although they may not express themselves in the same way as other children, they will still be grieving the person who has died. Just because they may not show any emotion doesn't mean they're not hurting.

It may be harder for an autistic child to understand the finality of death and how to ask for help. Those closest to the child will have the greatest understanding of their capabilities and will be best placed to explain things in an understandable way to the child. Using visual aids could prove useful. As an example, you could show them plants, flowers or leaves that have died.

General

All children, young, older, autistic or teens, will benefit from activities such as putting together a memory box, keeping photographs or something that reminds them of their loved one. It may also really help to involve them with funeral plans and ideas. Explaining what will happen and what they'll see.

Language is something that is really important. Use the correct, age-appropriate language, and avoid such phrases like 'gone to sleep', 'is a butterfly now' or 'lost'. These can all be so harmful. If you tell a small child that we've lost grandad, they may try to find him! The best way is to always be honest.

Children of all ages will have questions. There's going to be a lot they don't understand. Answer their questions as honestly as you can. If you don't know the answer to something, let them know and see if you can find out the answer together. Maybe the person(s) helping to arrange the funeral would be able to help. Maybe someone else in the family might have the answer.

Explain to them what will happen at the funeral. Especially if it's the first one they have attended. With such a crossover of American TV, children may expect to see an open coffin. They may not know the format, dress code or who will be there. It will be a difficult day for them anyway. The more you can prepare them, the less scary it will be. Explain that they may see people upset but that's ok.

Try not to make decisions for them or they may resent this later in life. A lot of these decisions will depend on their age and relationship with the deceased. Ask if they want to be involved.

Grief can affect a child's appetite, sleep pattern, memory and concentration. There are many useful resources available from books to information on child bereavement websites. The NHS has a section for 'bereavement and young people' which is full of information that will help.

Children may also develop a fear that others close to them may leave or die too. Letting them know you're still there, you'll be collecting them from school, or what your plan throughout the day is - even if it's three loads of washing and a food shop - will help them. Voiced normality and routine can act as a great reassurance.

Children look to those around them as to how to deal with situations and challenges in life. A bereavement is no different. They will model their behaviour on what they see. If the adults around them cover up their emotions, the children will think they need to do the same. This can lead to ongoing mental health problems for years after their loved one died. As a society we are often guilty of apologising if we cry, or stopping ourselves along with that apology. Let them see you cry so they know that this is normal. Set a good example and be open with them about your own feelings.

Children, as with adults, will go through a whole range of emotions. They need to know that this is ok. It's ok to feel sad; just as much as it's ok to feel happy. When they go back to school, it's fine to play with friends and socialise. It's fine to want to feel normal without feeling guilty. There is no set pattern with grief, and everyone will do it their own way and in their own time.

To some children, the routine of school, after school clubs, parties and play dates may be helpful. Children used to a routine will take comfort in that. It doesn't mean they're not grieving.

Ensure you notify school and ask that the information is shared amongst staff. If teachers and staff are unaware of what has happened, changes in behaviour can be seen as a negative and the school will act accordingly. If the deceased was an emergency contact, request that their details be removed from the system.

Although the age-appropriate understanding has been listed in this way, it is a guide and we recognise that every child is unique.

If you feel your child may need additional support, speak to their school again, contact your GP or seek out a local bereavement charity.

Tools for Resilience

In addition to open and honest conversations, providing children with effective tools for resilience can support their emotional wellbeing and help them develop healthy coping mechanisms, empowering them to navigate the challenges of grief and loss in a healthy and adaptive manner. These tools not only support their emotional wellbeing during the grieving process but also lay the foundation for their long-term resilience and ability to cope with adversity throughout their lives.

Supporting Emotional Expression: Grief can evoke a wide range of emotions such as sadness, anger, confusion, and even guilt. It is necessary to create a safe and non-judgmental space where children can freely express these emotions, openly and honestly. Encouraging them to talk about their feelings, whether through conversations, art, or writing, helps them process their emotions and develop a healthy emotional vocabulary.

Validating Emotions: It is important to let them know that their feelings are normal and understandable. We help them feel seen and understood when we acknowledge their emotions. Validating their emotions also helps them build trust and develop a sense of self-worth, knowing that their experiences and feelings are valid and valued.

Encouraging Self-Care: Grief can be physically and emotionally exhausting, and it is necessary to teach children the importance of taking care of themselves. Encourage them to engage in activities that bring them joy and comfort, such as spending time in nature, practicing mindfulness or relaxation techniques, pursuing hobbies, or engaging in physical exercise. Prioritising self-care, including their diet and cleanliness, sleep and rest, will help children learn to nurture their wellbeing and develop healthy habits to cope with the challenges of grief.

Building a Support Network: A strong support network can play a central role in encouraging resilience. Urge children to seek support from trusted adults, such as family members, teachers, counsellors, or support groups specifically designed for children experiencing loss. These individuals can provide guidance, validation, and a listening ear during difficult times. Additionally, connecting with peers who have experienced similar losses can be particularly beneficial, as it creates a sense of belonging and normalises their experiences.

Promoting Meaning-Making: Encourage them to explore activities that bring a sense of meaning, such as engaging in acts of kindness, volunteering, or participating in memorial events. By feeling a sense of purpose, children can find solace in honouring their loved ones' memories and contributing to something meaningful.

Teaching Healthy Coping Mechanisms: Support them in exploring various coping strategies, such as journaling, practicing deep breathing exercises, engaging in creative outlets like art or music, putting together a memory box, or seeking professional help when needed. It would help to emphasise that seeking help is a sign of strength and not a sign of weakness. Providing them with a range of healthy coping mechanisms empowers children to choose strategies that work best for them.

Clare's Story

I fell into writing by accident really. My husband had been working away for a few months and my children were missing him dreadfully. In a quiet moment, I wrote them a poem, which in turn became my first published book.

While promoting the book within schools, I had the perfect opportunity to discuss bereavement resources with the teachers. I had toyed with the idea of writing something to help but, at that point, wasn't sure how needed it was. I write from the child's perspective, in a very direct and straightforward manner, and this was something the teachers said was very much needed and they were excited about. Every one of them encouraged me wholeheartedly to go for it!

Way back in 1990, I had just started secondary school and was busy getting to grips with friendship groups, classes, hormones and everything else that goes with this transition. It was the week leading up to Christmas, Tuesday 18th to be exact, I was in science class when someone from the office popped their head around the door and asked for me. I was told to gather my things and someone was on the way to collect me. My brother, Andrew, had been rushed to hospital.

Most of what happened over the next 36 hours is a bit of a blur but I vividly remember sitting with my grandma and sister when the call came through to tell us that my brother, Andrew, had died. It was just past midnight, the Christmas lights were on but the room was otherwise dark and we just sat. It was the 20th of December.

Looking back, at the tender age of eleven, I didn't really understand what was going on. Everything had happened so quickly. We had his funeral on Christmas Eve and everyone came back to our house to "celebrate". Once school was open again in January, everything went back to normal. But, it was never normal.

Dad went back to work, my sister was seventeen and headed back to college and mum was busy looking after her father who had terminal cancer. It was pretty lonely. The following Christmas, my maternal grandfather died. It was the 21st of December. Come January, everything went back to the new normal. Except, it was even less normal now than before.

I was lost and vulnerable and didn't know how to deal with what was happening. I became an easy target for some of the "less friendly" girls and had a horrible time going through school. I would hide my emotions from everyone. This happened for two reasons; the first - I'd once cried in front of my mum who had then cried herself and I was worried that I'd upset her. That by showing my emotions, I'd caused her to get upset. I didn't understand the enormity of what we were all going through and that this was a natural part of our shared grief. The second - two of the "less friendly" girls had approached me not long after my grandad had died and were being cruel about something. I don't remember the details fully but I know that what they said upset me, I cried and they both turned on me saying that I was always crying. I tried to explain that grandad had just died (which they already knew) but they just carried on. They didn't care.

I tried not to show anything after that. I buried everything. Pushed it as far down as it would go. I spent the next twenty years ruining relationships and friendships because I was so dreadfully insecure. I was desperate to feel loved and yet determined to ruin it when I was. It was almost as if I'd pressed a self-destruct button in my mid teens and let it continue through to adulthood.

Not having understood the death of my loved ones, and the grief that followed, I had terrible fears of being left, being abandoned. It's something that's taken my husband twenty years to calm in me. My anxiety levels are often through the ceiling and in my late thirties, I had a breakdown that led me to a therapist. She worked with me to help me grieve for Andrew. So many of my mental health problems stemmed from not dealing with his death at the time. And definitely not dealing with the compounded grief that came when my grandad died. I have been so much better since going through this process. It made me determined to help children in similar situations not repeat what had happened to me. Having already published my first book, and with the backing of so many teaching professionals, I wrote Love Will Never Die; Helping Children Through Bereavement.

I have met children and families who have used this book after someone they love has died and the feedback is phenomenal. Knowing that I can help children - and their families - to open up and talk more about what's happened is such an amazing feeling. I never want any child to go through what I went through.

Working with John on this project has really inspired me. He is so passionate about getting people talking about death. To normalise those conversations. I couldn't agree more and jumped at this chance. I'm excited about what the future holds.

For Families

Grief is a deeply personal and complex experience that affects individuals of all ages. When it comes to children and families, having good methods for coping with grief is fundamental in helping them navigate this challenging journey together.

Practical strategies for children and families to cope with grief:

Coping with grief involves finding healthy ways to express emotions, process thoughts, and adjust to life after the loss of a loved one. As we know, for children, age-appropriate activities can play a significant role in their healing process. Drawing, painting, or engaging in play therapy can serve as outlets for self-expression and provide a sense of control over their emotions. Journaling can also be a helpful tool, allowing children to document their feelings and memories as they navigate their own grief journey. This can be hugely beneficial for adults too.

Be ready for all the "firsts" - first birthday, holiday, anniversary and so on. Families can establish rituals or traditions that honour the memory of their loved one. This might include lighting a candle, creating memory boxes, or dedicating a special space for reflection and remembrance. Engaging in physical activities together, such as walks or exercises, can help release emotions and promote a sense of togetherness. By encouraging open communication within the family, children and their parents or caregivers can share their feelings, memories, and stories, developing a supportive environment for healing.

Your time together may not always be about discussing your grief or the person who has died, but just be about spending time in each other's company. Cementing the family bond and appreciating the comfort of knowing that you're all there to support each other. It may be as simple as an opportunity to sit and watch a film together, or just enjoying family dinner with a bit of chatter and a giggle - without feeling guilty for doing so or for not mentioning your loved one.

Emotional support networks and professional resources:

Building a strong emotional support network can be really important for individuals coping with grief. This network can consist of family members, close friends, support groups, or professional counsellors. These individuals provide a listening ear, understanding, and empathy. Sharing experiences and emotions with others who have gone through similar situations can be comforting and validating.

In addition to personal support networks, professional resources are available to provide guidance and specialised assistance. Organisations such as Child Bereavement UK and Project Eileen play a significant role in offering support to children and families coping with grief. These charities offer a range of resources, including helplines, online forums, workshops, and counselling services tailored to meet the unique needs of bereaved individuals. Their expertise in child bereavement ensures that families receive appropriate guidance and assistance throughout the grieving process. Details for both organisations can be found at the end of the book.

Promoting self-care and seeking help when needed:

Grief can take a toll on both the physical and emotional wellbeing of most individuals. Promoting self-care practices is essential in maintaining overall health during the grieving process. Encouraging individuals to maintain regular sleep patterns, engage in physical activity, and to eat a balanced diet can support their physical wellbeing. Additionally, practicing relaxation techniques, such as deep breathing, meditation, or mindfulness exercises, can help manage stress and promote emotional wellbeing.

It is important to emphasise that seeking help is not a sign of weakness but a courageous step toward healing. Professional help, such as therapy or counselling, can provide additional guidance and support. Therapists specialising in grief and bereavement can offer individuals and families a safe space to express their feelings, explore coping strategies, and navigate the challenges that arise during the grieving process. By seeking professional help, individuals can gain valuable insights and tools to cope with their grief effectively.

Cultivating Gratitude in Daily Life:

Harnessing the practice of gratitude for life is an invitation to shift our focus from what we have lost to what we still have, and to cultivate a deep appreciation for the present moment.

When we are faced with loss and grief, it can be easy to get caught up in the past, longing for what was or dwelling on the emotional pain. However, by redirecting our attention to the here and now, we open ourselves up to the beauty and blessings that surround us. Whether it is the warmth of the sun on our skin, the laughter of loved ones, or the simple pleasures of everyday life, there is always something to be grateful for in the present moment. Focus on what you can do, rather than dwelling on what you can't.

Cultivating gratitude in daily life goes hand in hand with appreciating the present moment (mindfulness). It involves consciously shifting our perspective and actively seeking out moments of gratitude throughout our day. This can be done through simple practices such as keeping a gratitude journal, where we write down three things we are grateful for each day, or taking a few moments each morning to reflect on what we appreciate about our lives. By making gratitude a habit, we train our minds to focus on the positive aspects of life, even amidst the challenges of grief.

At the dinner table each evening, Clare's family take turns in sharing a positive from the day. Some days it can feel like there are no positives to share but we are encouraged to find something - even if it's something as simple as "I made it through work today". There are other days when we can list five or six positive things! It sounds simple (maybe even a little silly) but it's very effective. It took a little while to get into the habit but we all look for something positive every day now that we can share at dinnertime. We have all noticed a significant shift in our mindset.

Mindfulness:

Mindfulness is the practice of being fully present and engaged in the current moment. It involves paying attention to our thoughts, emotions, and sensations without judgment and quietening our brains. There are many websites and apps that can guide you when starting to use mindfulness.

Adult colouring is also a great way to unwind and focus your mind. As with any new habit, give it some time and persevere. We've added a few pages throughout the book to give examples.

When applied to the experience of grief, mindfulness allows us to be fully present with our emotions and to navigate them with compassion and understanding. It helps us to cultivate a deeper awareness of our inner world and to respond to grief with kindness and acceptance.

Finding joy and meaning during times of grief is not about denying or diminishing the pain of loss, but rather about seeking moments of joy, connection, and purpose that can coexist alongside grief.

Turning Darkness into Light: The Power of Resilience and Transforming Grief into Personal Growth

Grief is an inevitable part of the human experience. It casts a shadow over our lives, leaving us feeling lost, broken, and overwhelmed. Yet, within the depths of sorrow, lies the potential for transformation.

Each person's grief is deeply personal and unique, shaped by their own individual circumstances and relationships. Yet, it is a shared experience that unites us all as human beings. We have all faced loss, whether it be the passing of a loved one, the end of a relationship, or the loss of a cherished dream. It is in acknowledging this universal nature of loss that we find solace and connection. We are not alone in our grief.

Resilience is the key that unlocks the potential for personal growth. It is the capacity within each of us to bounce back, to adapt, and to find strength in the face of adversity. Resilience is not an innate trait; it is a skill that can be cultivated and nurtured.

Turning darkness into light begins with acknowledging and honouring the pain of loss. It is a process of allowing ourselves to feel the depths of sorrow, to sit with the darkness without judgment or haste. It is through this courageous act of facing our pain that we begin to heal and find the seeds of personal growth.

It is not about forgetting or moving on from the loss, but rather integrating it into our lives in a way that allows us to thrive. This transformation occurs through self-reflection, introspection, and finding meaning in our experiences. It is about discovering the lessons that grief has to teach us and using those lessons to shape our lives in a more profound and purposeful way, finding our own unique path, guided by our values, beliefs, and aspirations. It is not a linear journey, but rather a spiral of growth that evolves over time. It requires patience, self-compassion, and a willingness to embrace the complexities of our emotions.

May this book serve as a source of comfort, support, and inspiration for those navigating the challenging terrain of grief. Remember, you have the capability to find strength in the midst of sorrow, and to emerge from the depths of grief with renewed purpose and resilience.

As you embark on your own personal journey, it is essential to remember that healing is not a destination to be reached, but a continuous process of growth and self-discovery. Give yourself permission to grieve, to feel the full spectrum of emotions that accompany loss. Allow yourself the space and time to honour your loved ones and the impact they have had on your life.

Seek out support networks and resources that resonate with you. Whether it is joining a grief support group, reaching out to a therapist or counsellor, or finding solace in the wisdom of others who have walked a similar path, remember that you do not have to face grief alone.

In your journey of turning darkness into light, be gentle with yourself. Practice self-care and self-compassion, recognising that healing takes time and that it is ok to take breaks when needed. Engage in activities that bring you joy and provide moments of respite from the weight of grief. Nurture your physical, emotional, and spiritual wellbeing, understanding that caring for yourself is an essential part of the healing process.

As you navigate the complexities of grief, remember that there is no right or wrong way to grieve, and what works for one individual may not work for another. Honour your own process and give yourself permission to find your own path. Embrace the lessons that grief has to offer, allowing them to shape your perspective and guide you towards personal growth.

Finally, remember that even in the darkest moments, there is light. Within the depths of grief, there is an opportunity for profound self-discovery, strength, and resilience. Embrace the power within you to turn your pain into purpose, your sorrow into compassion, and your loss into a catalyst for positive change.

You are not defined by your grief, but by the way you navigate it and transform it into something meaningful. May your journey be filled with healing, growth, and a profound sense of self-empowerment.

Notes

Notes

Notes

Part 2

Death and the Funeral

Creating Connection Points

When a loved one passes away, it is helpful to involve children in the funeral arrangements and rituals (if they choose to), as this can have a positive impact in their grieving process. **Creating connection points** - moments at which they are connected to their loved one - allows children to have a sense of ownership and participation, honouring their relationship with the deceased and facilitating their healing journey.

Having open conversations with children about death and involving them in funeral arrangements can help prevent the development of unresolved anger in the future. When children are given the opportunity to express their emotions, ask questions, and actively participate, they are more likely to feel heard and understood.

Including children in the funeral planning process can help them feel connected and involved. This involvement can range from simple tasks like choosing flowers, selecting music, or creating memorial artwork. By participating, children can express their love and contribute to creating a meaningful farewell that reflects their unique relationship with the deceased.

Allowing children to place pictures, letters, or cherished items in the coffin can provide a tangible connection to their loved one. These items hold deep sentimental value and symbolise their ongoing bond. Placing such mementos can offer a sense of comfort and provide an opportunity for children to express their emotions, share final messages, or preserve memories. It also allows them to see their loved one at rest. This could help with their understanding and acceptance of death.

If they choose not to view their loved one's body, **viewing the closed coffin** can be a significant step in the grieving process for children. It provides them with a chance to say goodbye, to witness the physical reality of death, and to begin accepting the finality of their loss. Viewing the closed coffin can help validate their emotions, create closure, and facilitate the understanding that death is a natural part of life. It will also prepare them for the funeral as the coffin would usually be on display.

Including children in farewell rituals, such as memorial services or ceremonies, allows them to actively participate in remembering their loved one. This can involve reading a poem, sharing memories, or lighting a candle. Involving children in these rituals acknowledges their grief and provides them with an opportunity to express their emotions openly and publicly. It also helps normalise their experiences and reinforces the importance of collective support during times of loss.

By creating these connection points and involving children in funeral arrangements and rituals we empower future generations to develop resilience, compassion, and healthy coping mechanisms in the face of grief and loss.

What Happens When Someone Dies?

Practical and professional advice from John Adams

When someone dies at any location, it is really important to create a calming environment, not only for the deceased but for any family and friends who may be present at the death. Understanding what death looks like can help with this, but not many people have a vast amount of experience of this.

Being present in the moment is very important though as things can happen very quickly and suddenly, and you need to be prepared. When that person does eventually die, my advice is to always take your time in calling the funeral director to come and take care of that person. The time after someone dying can be a very special time, and allowing yourself time to reflect can have a profound impact on your grief as you move forward. I have experienced doctors who have instructed families to call the funeral director immediately to come and transfer their loved one into the funeral home. My advice is to take control of the situation and challenge this advice to do things at your speed in your time. It is important the bereaved do not feel their loved one now becomes part of clinical detached process where they are watching this new journey at a distance.

In March 2024, I looked after a family who wanted their loved one remaining at home until the day of the funeral. After twelve days at the family home, in his own bed, with further delays anticipated due to availability of the local vicar, the family eventually decided that their loved one came into our care until the day of the funeral. From spending time with the family following frequent visits, those twelve days with the loved one remaining at home in his bed helped them so much understand and accept that he had died. When we talk about connection points in this book, this example, which would not be right for the majority of people, went on to have a profoundly positive impact for the family. On the day of the funeral, children were present at the family home when we returned the coffin one last time and removed the lid for all to spend some final time with their loved one. The children even helped me place the coffin lid on when it came to the time of departing the family home. Again, with age-appropriate communication, spoken with care and honesty there was no sadness or fear amongst the house, only love, calmness and full awareness of what was happening.

What is the process?

When someone dies at their home address, prior to calling your funeral director, the family must contact the medical professional who looked after the deceased during their last illness. As soon as the initial notification of death has been completed by a medical professional, and they have issued a medical certificate confirming the cause of death, the funeral director may attend the location.

If the deceased had no medical issues, and the death was sudden or unexpected (for example, finding someone unresponsive) usually the first responders, police or ambulance will arrive at the scene first. Depending on what has happened, the funeral director who carries out duties on behalf of HM Coroner will be called to take care of the person who has died and transfer them into HM Coroners custody. If this is the case, you will be told why this is needed and when to expect the medical certificate. There will be a faster time response to attend the location if the death was sudden or unnatural (ie suicide, road traffic incident etc) which will be out of the funeral director's control. When the Coroner is involved, they and their team should update the next of kin on the course of action at every stage. When clearance has been granted the funeral director will be notified and at that stage the deceased can then be taken into the funeral home mortuary.

On arrival at the funeral home from any location, the funeral operatives will ensure the deceased is 'checked in' to their funeral home mortuary, logging any personal items with the deceased and ensuring identification of the person is recorded in the mortuary register. It is also vitally important the deceased have identification attached to them in the form of a wristband (many funeral directors will place an additional ID band on the ankle as well), this will show their full name, date of birth, date of death and the location of death. The deceased will be covered in a dignified way. Some funeral directors will place moisturiser on the face and hands of the deceased as soon as they arrive into their care, this will help with the hydration of the skin which naturally will start to deteriorate as time moves forward. Embalming can also help with slowing down this natural process and make the experience of seeing your loved one much more positive. Embalming is a personal choice for the family to make and should be discussed with the funeral director.

How do I register a death?

Once you have the medical certificate mentioned above, you will need to make an appointment at your local register office (the office of the Registrar for Births and Deaths). This needs to be done within five days of the death (eight in Scotland). They will issue you with the documents needed to arrange the funeral. The gov.uk website has full details of what documents you will need to take with you.

When advising companies about your loved one's death, they will request to see an original copy of the death certificate. It is recommended that you request between five and ten copies depending on how many banks or financial companies (insurance/pension) you're dealing with.

If someone dies in hospital, how long is it until they move to the chosen funeral director?

Funeral directors can collect deceased from hospital mortuaries when the family have registered the death and the funeral director has received the certificate for burial or cremation (green in colour). If cremation has been chosen, the Cremation Form 4 will also be required to be completed (at the time of writing 2023/24), prior to being allowed to attend the hospital. More and more hospitals are now requiring additional documents which they have created themselves prior to the funeral directors being allowed to collect the deceased. This process can take a few days.

Funeral Choices

Your funeral director will guide you through the various choices that you have available to you in regard to coffins, flowers and how you want the funeral to happen. You may feel that you have no idea! Do not feel under any pressure to make snap decisions. My guidance to funeral arrangers is to always try and learn about the person who has died. By doing so they will be able to offer more personalised suggestions.

Some of the most incredible funeral arrangements I have been involved in are where I have been creative in order to meet the wishes of the family and their loved one. If the person making the funeral arrangements seems in doubt, my advice is to always have more space and time to decide what feels right.

The most ideal solution would be to have had the discussion pre-death. The idea of open conversations around death and dying could also help enormously when it comes to planning a funeral. It would be far easier to know someone's wishes in advance. What songs they would choose. What flowers they loved the most. Some people even plan the whole of their funeral in advance - what an amazing idea! If you feel open to discussing it, planning could make things that little bit easier when the time comes. Clare's mum has had a list of songs she wants played at her funeral for over a decade. She's still, very much, alive and kicking!

Memorials

There are many ways in which you can memorialise your loved ones. Aside from traditional graves within a cemetery or crematorium, you can have your loved one's ashes made into jewellery or a garden ornament. You can even have your loved one's ashes sent into space!

There are natural burial grounds around the country that offer spaces in a forest, wood or meadow as a place of rest.

Funeral directors are able to take fingerprints of the deceased which can be used for fingerprint jewellery. Locks of hair can also be obtained when requested and used as keepsakes. It could be worth considering these options before your final goodbye.

Administration

You will need to notify all companies in receipt of Direct Debits or standing orders (utilities, mobile phone etc) of the death and provide a copy of the death certificate (certified copy of an entry). You will need to contact all banks who the deceased held accounts with. These will all be frozen once notified but the majority of banks will still release money from a frozen account to pay for a funeral. They will just need to see the invoice from the funeral director and will often make a direct transfer on behalf of the next of kin.

Some people choose to have a "When I'm Gone" file that is kept with someone they trust, either electronically or in paper form. This file lists all accounts, pensions, insurances and anything useful that may need to be accessed following their death.

The online platform Life Ledger (lifeledger.com) are a notifying service that can inform over 1,000 UK companies, ranging from banks, insurers and pension providers to gas, water, telecoms and social media. This is free of charge to use and will save much time and energy during such a stressful period for the bereaved.

If the person was still working, or in receipt of any benefits or pensions, all organisations will need to be informed. Life Ledger can again carry out these notifications and you can check the progress at any time.

Paying for the Funeral

In July 2022, pre paid funeral plans become regulated by the Financial Conduct Authority (FCA). The list of plan providers can be found on FCA website (fca.org.uk) or online at the National Association of Funeral Plan Providers (nafpp.org). Payments to funeral directors from plan providers should be transferred immediately on the plan provider receiving proof of death, usually through the funeral director sending a copy of the Certificate of Burial or Cremation.

With insurance companies, the time waiting to receive payment will vary, again they will require proof of death through the form of the Certificate of Burial or Cremation or through a certified copy of an entry (Death Certificate) Please note, some insurance companies may have different requirements prior to money being released.

All funeral directors are legally required to publish a price list for their standard set of products and services.

Wills and Estates

Another uncomfortable conversation for people is around a person's estate - all of their worldly possessions and wealth. We have seen too many families destroyed following a death because of disagreements surrounding the contents of a will, or there being no will at all.

Siblings and step-siblings battling in court for months and years, and never speaking again. Or the classic family disputes when a partner is left the estate in good faith, only to change their will once the partner dies to leave everything to their own family and not that of the deceased. Having a well written will, and discussing your wishes with relatives, could go some way to avoiding something similar happening to your family.

Some situations may be impossible to avoid so any conversations about these things can be helpful to have while still alive. It may be a piece of jewellery that you'd like to leave to a certain family member - make sure it's written down. Ensure that it has been discussed with the wider family. A child grieving for their mother, expecting a promised trinket, could react very badly to finding out it's been given to someone else. If the rest of the family don't know, mistakes can happen. If it's written in the will, or been talked about in advance, there's a chance it can be rectified.

For families with younger children, a will is also extremely important in legally noting who would have guardianship of your children in the event of your death. This is not something that young families want to think about, and something that most likely will never need to be actioned, but knowing they're going to be cared for by a trusted friend of family member of your/their choosing if the unthinkable happens can offer peace of mind.

There are many organisations that offer a free will writing service. You can also find a large amount of information on the Citizens Advice website - citizensadvice.org.uk.

Power of Attorney

Power of attorney is a legal process where you appoint someone else to act on your behalf should you become too poorly to make decisions. A power of attorney gives the nominated person the legal authority to deal with finances, such as bill paying and banking. Some types of power of attorney also give the nominated person the legal power to make a decision on behalf of someone else when it comes to medical needs and care. To find out more about the various options and how to go through the process, visit the Citizens Advice website.

Notes

Q&A with John Adams

Over the years, John has been asked many questions. Some that people deem "silly" and some that people wished they'd asked at the time but didn't. We have covered a selection here that may prove useful.

How do I tell a child someone has died?

Honesty is the best policy. As a society I believe we struggle telling children about death, not just because we want to prevent upset, but because we naturally want to protect young people. Having these conversations as adults can be difficult enough, especially when someone we loved has died.

Use age-appropriate language while ensuring that you use the correct terminology, such as died rather than "slipped away" or "lost". Using these words can cause further confusion for young people. Being clear and honest, but speaking with kindness and care will have the most positive outcome.

Should all children attend funerals?

Every person and child are unique, therefore the decision of whether a child should attend the funeral will always be individual. My advice is to always talk with the child, honest conversations are critical. In the future children will always remember their voices were listened to and that they mattered.

Should a child be involved in a burial?

One way young people can be involved without any pressure is to take the middle lowers webs (the middle handles of the coffin), this means they do not have any responsibility in taking any weight of the coffin, but symbolically they can be involved in lowering which can be a very powerful connection point.

As we discuss throughout the book though, this may be too much for some children and all bereaved (of any age) will have different needs and requirements. The key area is they are aware they can be involved in this special act if they choose to.

Traditionally, mourners will be offered committal earth which they can place on the coffin once the coffin has been interred. There is also the option to place flower petals into the grave which can have the same purpose but is much softer than earth/soil - especially when young people are involved.

There can be concerns from children about insects getting into the coffin once burial has taken place. To reassure families and children, I will explain that many insects are unable to reach the depth of a coffin in the ground. In the past this has really helped and provided much needed reassurance.

Is it easier to not have a funeral with the increased prevalence of direct unattended cremation?

The UK is seeing a shift away from a traditional funeral service, the most recent census (2022) shows over half of the UK population are now non religious. The statistic will influence funeral services. However, I believe we need to change our approach on what a funeral service is. A funeral service needs to be about creating a space and connection for the bereaved to move forward with their grief. The more personal we can make this, with increased connection points carried out, the more healthy the bereaved will move forward with their loss.

It has been years and I do not feel like I have move forward with my grief, what should I do?

We are all unique, therefore we all grieve differently. My advice is to carry out activities to ensure you have truly dealt with your grief. This can involve thinking about the person and recognising the emotions this brings forth. If you would normally try to stop crying or feeling sad when the person is thought of, change this. When you cry for the person, acknowledge that this is what you're doing. This can help you to process your grief and start to allow yourself to heal.

If you are struggling with your grief in the long term and feel like it is having a marked impact on your life, then it might help to talk to your GP or seek professional bereavement support.

You talk about connection points, what is the affect if I do not want any connection with my loved one?

At a time of loss, we can often find ourselves being caught up in a combination of emotions. The decisions we make at that time may have long affects on our grief and our journey to move forward in a positive way. My advice would be to not just look at what you need right now, but look at what connection points might help with your grief and life in ten years from now. I have met families who opted for an unattended direct cremation for their loved ones, this was done to try and save the family from the pain of going through their loss. One year on that same family are having a difficult time in acknowledging and accepting the death even took place. Being mindful for the future is critical.

I did not love nor like my family member who died, what consideration should be taken when this is encountered?

I would suggest you explore within yourself if you still need to say goodbye. Despite the feelings towards a person, the funeral service may be an opportunity to have that space to forgive them or forgive yourself. Difficult moments can also be the most important ones.

Can I bring a pet to a funeral?

Yes, providing the venue at which the service is carried out allows. I was shocked to learn that Westerleigh Crematorium allowed a horse into one of their Crematorium chapels. This proves the point that a funeral should be personalised to what that specific family need for their loved one. Also, a family pet may have had more interaction with the deceased than any human.

Why is it important to talk about funeral wishes in advance?

Uncomfortable conversations are usually the most important ones. I have arranged many funerals when the person carrying out the funeral arrangements has no idea of what the person who has died would want. The alternative is arranging a funeral with all wishes in place, there is no guess work and you have a platform to work from. A site we have recently created to assist with this **legacyshare.co.uk**, to enable important conversations and store your funeral wishes and legacy. As well as asking questions on funeral wishes, this site is also an educational tool for society. The service is free to use.

I do not want a funeral when I die, what can I do to ensure this happens?

Place this down in your funeral wishes and speak with anyone left behind in the reason why. This can help in the future with any anguish in relatives not having that opportunity. The question I would ask you would be, will it affect anyone in a negative way in you not having a funeral or a space for someone to say goodbye? Could you look at other ways to create connection points?

There is also the opportunity to give your body to science; applications for this must be completed in advance and further details can be found on the human tissue authority website.

Baby loss is not talked about in the UK, why is there such a stigma around this?

This can often be a difficult area for society to discuss. With any loss communication can be challenging, and with a loss of a baby it can be even more difficult for family and friends to offer support. Our interview with Steph Wild from Beyond Bea can be found on our podcast, Death a Changing Industry (achangingindustry.com), where we go in great depth on the affects of baby loss and the services around this. Support suppliers such as CuddleCot (flexmort.com/cuddle-cot) are really pushing the societal boundaries on baby loss and are also contributing in making a positive change.

Why can't we let children be children and wait for them to learn about this when they are older?

Death is all around us, we cannot avoid the only guarantee in life. Children have so many questions around this; I have spoken at schools and have personally witnessed empowerment of young people around death. The thought of death can be associated with fear, fear is manifested from the unknown. Remove the unknown and it may help reduce the fear!

What is embalming?

Embalming will be carried out to improve the presentation of the deceased, assist with a more hygienic environment and to also help with the preservation of that person, as after death our bodies will naturally break down. The rate of the breakdown will always vary as we are all unique. There are factors that will increase the deterioration of a body such as various medications and the environment in which someone has died. Refrigeration within a funeral home can assist in maintaining the deceased presentation and preservation.

The embalmer, who should be qualified with the British Institute of Embalmers, will prepare a bespoke embalming solution, depending on the needs of the deceased, and introduce this into the arterial network of the body. Embalming can also be carried out when a loved one is not being seen but when trying to assist in reducing the risk of bacteria spreading. The funeral director should always obtain permission to embalm and advise if embalming will be beneficial.

I do not like the idea of embalming - why does this need to take place?

Embalming does not need to take place as a mandatory requirement. Every person is unique therefore the methods and the need to embalm should also be case by case. It can help when going to spend time and see your loved one. It can also help when there is a long gap from the date of death until the date of the funeral. Seeing your loved one in the chapel of rest may be very helpful, this will help accept the death has happened and can act as an important connection point. Spending time in the chapel of rest with the coffin closed can also help create connection and is not as stark as actually seeing your loved one. This can also be a helpful suggestion when children are involved and would like to attend the chapel of rest. It also allows those attending the funeral to see the coffin prior to the day of the funeral, removing any shock from the day itself.

How do I describe cremation to a child?

From my experience of explaining cremation to children, I have talked about the crematorium being a special venue and space where we go to say goodbye to our loved ones. I will explain the goodbye is only physical, as love and emotion will live on for a lifetime. When discussing cremated remains (ashes) I describe how the crematorium have a special facility there, which uses a special heat and flame, which will then transform us from our current body form into a very special powder called ashes. We need to remember that despite looking very different to our current body form, these ashes are very important and should be shown the utmost respect at all times.

I used the above example when a lady called me at my funeral home for advice on how to speak to her granddaughter who was unsure whether she should attend the interment of her grandad's ashes at a local cemetery the following week. Prior to giving any advice, I asked if the granddaughter actually wanted to attend the interment, how old she was, and what communication had been used to explain the interment so far. Unfortunately, and with the best intentions, the family had told the granddaughter, who was aged around 10, that grandad had been shrunken down to a miniature version of himself to fit in the Cremated Remains casket. For those unsure, this is a shoe box sized container! They explained that following this communication she now seemed very confused.

The family were trying their best to protect the granddaughter who they loved very much. However, by creating this idea of her grandad now the size of a Russian doll it may have caused more damage and confusion as time moved forward.

Only a few days after receiving the phone call, I spent time with the granddaughter, with her mother and grandmother present. I talked with her about the crematorium process in an age-appropriate way, with kindness, care and honesty. The relief of the elders in the room was very apparent, and to the granddaughter it was all very simple. No trauma or no sadness whatsoever.

What could have been very helpful in preparing this young person for the interment would have been to show her the location where the burial was set to take place in advance of the day. This also applies for showing young people and some adults the crematorium or other funeral venues, doing this can help relieve pressure and built up fear on the day of a service.

When my Mum died, we chose not to remove her wedding ring. What happens to this once she's been cremated?

If the family had opted to have a ring or any other personal items remain on the deceased for cremation then they will also be cremated. The items will be melted down and removed from the cremator when collecting all the cremated remains of that person. All metals, including melted down jewellery, replacement joints and metals for the construction of the coffin, will be collected for the metal recycling scheme. The metals are separated, melted down and sold, with the profits going back to the crematorium. However, the money they receive must go to charity, therefore benefiting the local community.

When arranging the funeral, my advice is to ask the family if they intend to inter the cremated remains at a later date. If a burial of the cremated remains is their intention, then my suggestion would be to remove any personal jewellery with the deceased to later place in the ashes casket in the items full form. Doing this, the items will remain intact and remain with that person.

Where can I hold a funeral?

With consent, a funeral service can be held anywhere. As society moves forward and continues to become less religious (based on the recent census) funeral arrangers can show creativity in offering more to families in terms of the space used and personalisation. The word personalisation is used a lot. For me, true personalisation does not cost anything. For example, I suggested a family return their loved one to the stables she loved prior to the funeral. We placed her coffin in the centre of the stables, where I witnessed her horse placing his head on the coffin. This was more powerful than any prop we can provide and again gave the family a true connection point which will stay with them forever.

You mention putting items into the coffin, are there any restrictions?

Yes, for cremation they need to be of natural material. With burial there are fewer restrictions. I have even seen someone place a cat they had just put down in their loved one's coffin. Other items we've come across include fishing rods, pictures, letters and drawings.

Are the deceased always kept at the funeral home or moved back and forth for viewings from a central mortuary?

The deceased are usually kept at one funeral home and that is where you will have the option to see and spend time with your loved one. If transporting to different locations is required, then this should be communicated to the families at all times. Families have a right to know where their loved one is at all times.

If I am not happy with my chosen funeral director, can I move my loved one elsewhere?

Yes, if families are uncomfortable with the service being provided a conversation needs to happen. By law you have 14 days to make a decision. Prior to choosing your funeral director, ask family and friends for recommendations, look online for reviews and if you are able to, ask the funeral directors if you may visit their facility. A good funeral director will be comfortable showing you their mortuary space and, of course, you would not see any deceased whilst carrying out this inspection. This request should not require a vast amount of time to arrange.

Is the Funeral industry regulated?

Both NAFD and SAIF (The National Society of Allied and Independent Funeral Directors) carry out regular inspections on their members, but the industry as a whole is not currently regulated. It is my belief that in the near future the funeral industry will become fully regulated. This is based on the intervention of the Competition Market Authority (CMA) enforcing rulings on funeral directors to display pricelists online and within the funeral home to provide price transparency.

What we have seen from these enforcements is that the funeral industry has many aspects to the services provided to the public - how we measure and continuously monitor this is not straight forward. Overall though, I believe tighter regulation will be a positive step to ensure more consistency throughout the funeral industry.

Questions Children Ask

I was recently invited into a local primary school to speak with the pupils following the death of one of their teachers. I attended with my colleague, Kirstie Hurst-Knight, from Shropshire Council. Rather than a whole school assembly, we were asked to visit each classroom and talk to the children in smaller groups.

I spoke about the funeral the following day and, despite this being a hard day, why it was so important. I showed them the top hat that I would be wearing and explained that, even though I may look slightly different, it would still be 'their new friend, John' looking after their teacher on the day. I also took a toy hearse and showed the classes what their teacher's coffin would look like.

I asked every class if they could help me to make the family a present to show how much love there is for their teacher. I gave all those wanting to take part a small wooden heart and we used an ink pad to press their fingerprints on the wooden hearts. On the day of the funeral, the cortege travelled to the school one last time. We presented the family with a surprise gift of a jar of hearts with a fingerprint of every child from the school. This act created a beautiful connection point. All children from the school were present on the playing field to take part.

I would like to take this opportunity to thank and commend the head teacher of this particular school, Mr. Bridges. His proactive approach was an example of how, with honest and careful communication, the community within the school was in a much better position to face a difficult situation.

I was asked a lot of questions by the children about what had happened and what was going to happen next. I have included a selection below.

Are her eyes open or closed?

I explained they were closed and this was important as we wanted to make the experience as peaceful as possible when their teachers family came to spend time with her in the chapel of rest.

When she died, where did she go?

I explained their teacher had been in my funeral home, and that I was personally responsible for making sure she was shown the utmost respect and care.

Who is looking after her children now?

This question was asked with real concern. My colleague and I explained that their teacher's two children had lots of family who were going to take great care of them.

Will we be able to see her tomorrow?

I explained that all the children will have the opportunity to see their teacher's coffin, but it was important they only saw the outside of the coffin, not the inside. This was out of respect for their teacher and her family who will be in the car behind the hearse tomorrow.

How did she die?

I talked about how their teacher got so seriously poorly that she died. We discussed that part of being alive is getting ill, we all get poorly from time to time and, on rare occasions, like when my mum died when I was twelve, people can die, 'pass away'. With this response a child put her hand up and said her grandmother got extremely poorly but now she is completely fine. I said that was the perfect example and added that I don't want anyone of them getting worried when them or their family get poorly. What has happened to their teacher is very rare, but sadly on extreme occasions can happen. The key is now we all pull together, with kindness and love.

Why do you wear a top hat?

I explained it is a tradition in my role, I am not overly keen on some traditions but wearing this helps people find me if they feel worried, sad or have a problem they need to talk about.

How does the coffin get into the hearse?

With this I explained the coffin has handles that are secured to the sides of the coffin, and that the team I work with at my funeral home will carry the coffin together and carefully place this onto the hearse. I also mentioned that the family of the special teacher will be carrying the coffin on the day of the funeral.

How many funerals have you done?

I told the class I had conducted many funerals and in the Royal Navy I was trained to look after Military personnel with their funerals if they died whilst serving in wars. I went on to say how important every funeral is that takes place and that's why at my young age I am now going grey!

How long have you been taking care of people?

I spoke about how I used to help wash the funeral cars when I was at school. I left school when I was sixteen to join my family funeral service but after twelve months decided I was too young to work there. I decided to join the Royal Navy where I spent eight years travelling all over the world, which was a really cool job. What I do now may seem sad to many people, but I feel so lucky and grateful to help people, especially young people, at a time which can be the most difficult in all of their lives. It is my belief the hardest time in your life can be turned over and become the fuel to help others live better lives.

The Role of the Funeral Director

The role of the funeral director is certainly getting more complex, especially as we see further regulation coming into the profession. However, the core values of what we do must always be about the genuine care we provide the bereaved and their loved ones who are entrusted into our care.

The funeral director has the responsibility and duty of providing a high standard of service throughout all their involvement. The small details all matter; from initially receiving the first call in a professional, friendly and efficient manner, to how we handle and take care of their loved one when bringing them into our charge, through to providing a professional but welcoming funeral home. With consistent communication there should be no guess work leading up to the day of the funeral, from music choices, the types of vehicles used and coffin choices. All the funeral team need to ensure they are presented correctly and respectfully.

The company culture of the funeral home is also very important. This is to ensure all members of the team truly understand the importance of why every funeral service we are involved in is a huge honour and privilege. Every detail matters and how we treat the deceased with the utmost respect and care when no one is watching, for me will always be a priority. Ceremony does form part of the role, but the most important role the funeral director has on the day is to lead and create the right environment to make a sad day special.

Funeral directors play a pivotal role in supporting families during their most vulnerable moments. By practicing compassion and empathy, funeral directors can create a safe and nurturing environment for the bereaved. This involves active listening, validating emotions, and providing gentle guidance throughout the funeral planning process. Funeral directors should aim to foster a sense of trust and understanding, allowing families to openly express their wishes, concerns, and preferences. Through demonstrating sensitivity and compassion, funeral directors can help alleviate some of the burdens and uncertainties that families may face during this challenging time.

Grief can be an overwhelming and complex journey, and families may require guidance and resources to navigate through it. Funeral directors can offer information and support regarding grief counselling services, support groups, and other resources available in the community. Connecting families with these resources, funeral directors empower them to seek additional assistance when needed and provide them with a network of support beyond the immediate funeral arrangements. This guidance helps families understand that they are not alone in their grief and that there are organisations that provide valuable support and resources tailored to their specific needs.

Many funeral directors hold stock of bereavement resources on site. For example, Clare's two titles, Love Will Never Die and A Mind Full of Grief, written for younger children and teenagers respectively. As the funeral directors are involved with the families very early in their grief journey, getting these resources to them in good time is invaluable.

Each family has unique cultural, religious, and personal practices when it comes to mourning and remembrance. Funeral directors should strive to create inclusive spaces that respect and accommodate these diverse needs. This can include providing options for different funeral rituals, allowing families to personalise ceremonies and memorial services, and being sensitive to cultural and religious customs. Embracing diversity and inclusivity, funeral directors ensure that families feel supported and that their loved ones are honoured and remembered in a way that aligns with their beliefs and traditions.

There are time sensitive tasks that need to be completed but funeral directors must try not to put pressure on the family. Creating a calm environment, where the bereaved feel in control over the arrangements is key. Many who are tasked with arranging a funeral will not necessarily be thinking straight, and having dozens of decisions to make every day will be overwhelming. The funeral director has the responsibility and duty of providing a high standard of service. An example is checking for errors on the order of service or invoices. This will all go a long way to alleviating some of the pressures to the family. Any simple, yet practical, help could make all the difference to a family. The role when arranging a funeral is changing, we need to show our creativity in ensuring it is the funeral service the family and their loved one wants, not what is convenient to us. Giving families choice when arranging a funeral is so important and we need to make suggestions based on what we learn about the deceased. The funeral service can only be done once, there is no second chance, therefore it must be right first time.

Through implementing compassionate practices for funeral directors, providing guidance and resources for families, and creating inclusive spaces for mourning and remembrance, we can offer comprehensive support to families as they navigate their grief journey. The involvement of organisations specialising in supporting bereaved families, such as Child Bereavement UK and Project Eileen, can further enhance the support available. These organisations have valuable expertise in providing assistance tailored to the needs of bereaved children and their families. Funeral directors can collaborate with these organisations to access additional support and ensure that families receive the care they need during the challenging process of grieving.

Part 3

For Professionals Working with Children

Learning About Death, Dying, and Bereavement in Schools

The impact of death and bereavement is profound, shaping our understanding of mortality and challenging our emotional wellbeing. In recognition of the significance of these topics, we believe there is a growing need for mandatory sessions on death, dying, and bereavement within schools.

Children learn about essential life skills through PSHE and RSE, covering "the importance of physical activity and diet for a healthy lifestyle", "drug, financial, sex and relationship education" and "an understanding of government, democracy and law". This is all to equip them with skills to take into society and live theirs lives in the best way possible. The one sure thing in life is death. Yet, it is not discussed within these boundaries.

It is essential to acknowledge that everyone will face loss at some point in their lives, as uncomfortable as that thought may be, whether it is the death of a loved one, a friend, or even a pet. By introducing education on death into schools in a thoughtful and sensitive manner, we provide children with a foundation of knowledge and understanding that can help them navigate these challenging times with greater resilience and empathy.

Currently, many educational institutions shy away from discussing death due to cultural taboos, fear of causing discomfort, or a lack of awareness about how to approach the subject with children. However, avoiding these conversations may inadvertently perpetuate misunderstandings and misconceptions about death, which can further contribute to the stigma surrounding grief. It also denies children the opportunity to develop the necessary skills and emotional intelligence to cope with loss effectively.

Another challenge is the diversity of cultural and religious beliefs surrounding death and mourning practices. It is essential to approach these discussions with cultural sensitivity and respect for individual beliefs and traditions. Similarly to Religious Education where discussions are held on the various festivals and celebrations each religion has. By incorporating diverse perspectives and fostering an atmosphere of inclusivity, we can create a learning environment that encourages understanding and empathy towards different ways of grieving and honouring the deceased.

Overcoming cultural and societal barriers to discussing death with children requires a shift in perspective and a commitment to open dialogue. It is essential to create an environment where children feel safe and supported in exploring their questions, fears, and emotions surrounding death. By providing age-appropriate information and facilitating discussions, we can empower children to develop a healthier relationship with death, helping them cope with loss when it inevitably occurs.

Introducing mandatory sessions on death, dying, and bereavement in schools, will provide children with the necessary tools to navigate the complexities of loss. These sessions can cover a range of topics, such as the emotional impact of grief, different cultural practices surrounding death, how to support grieving individuals, and coping strategies for navigating personal loss.

One of the significant benefits of introducing education on death and bereavement in schools is that it helps to normalise these conversations. Children are already exposed to death and grief through various channels, such as books, movies, news, and personal experiences. By providing structured and guided discussions within the school setting, we create a safe and supportive environment for children to process their emotions and gain a deeper understanding of death.

Furthermore, incorporating mandatory sessions on death and bereavement in the curriculum acknowledges the unique emotional needs of children. Children may experience grief differently from adults and may struggle to express their emotions or understand the complexities of loss. By tailoring the content and activities to their developmental level, we can effectively address their needs and empower them to navigate the grieving process.

These sessions can include age-appropriate explanations of death, discussions on common emotions experienced during grief, and strategies for coping with loss. By providing a vocabulary and framework for discussing death, children can develop the language skills necessary to express their feelings and seek support when needed. Moreover, engaging in activities that encourage emotional expression, such as art therapy or journaling, can help children process their emotions in a healthy and constructive manner.

Grief can be physically and mentally exhausting, and it is crucial to equip children with tools to take care of themselves during difficult times. This can involve teaching relaxation techniques, promoting healthy coping mechanisms like exercise or engaging in hobbies, and emphasising the importance of self-compassion and self-care routines.

John has made a significant step towards normalising discussions about death in schools with the success of a petition aimed at adding content on death, dying, and bereavement into the National Curriculum. With over 12,000 signatures obtained, this initiative has highlighted the growing recognition of the importance of addressing these topics in an educational setting. The petition's success demonstrates the collective desire to equip future generations with the knowledge and skills to navigate grief and loss in a healthy and informed manner.

On Wednesday 15th May 2024, John received notification from Parliament that the Petitions Committee had held a meeting to consider scheduling petitions with over 100K signatures for debate. The Committee sometimes schedules debates on petitions under this threshold, and were pleased to inform him that the Petitions Committee agreed to schedule a debate on two petitions about children and bereavement, including our petition to "Add content on death, dying and bereavement to the national curriculum". The other petition that will be debated alongside this is: Record the number of bereaved children to ensure they are supported.

The debate will take place on Monday 17th June in Westminster Hall. This was another huge step forward to achieving the overall goal.

Talking to the Children

In many societies, death is often seen as a taboo subject, shrouded in fear and silence. However, by breaking down these barriers and promoting open dialogue, we can create a supportive environment that normalises conversations about death and grief.

One of the first steps in breaking the taboo is to address the fear associated with death. Death is an inevitable part of life, yet it is often surrounded by anxiety and uncertainty. By providing accurate information and dispelling misconceptions, we can alleviate some of these fears and help children develop a more realistic understanding of death.

Educational sessions on death and bereavement should provide children with age-appropriate and factual information. This may include explaining the biological processes of death, the concept of mortality, and the different causes of death. If we demystify death and provide scientific explanations, we can help children develop a more rational and informed perspective.

Death is so often portrayed as a painful and agonising experience in films and on television programmes. It's no wonder children (and adults!) could be scared. For most, death is a very peaceful process.

Some children may also have misconceptions that death is contagious or that dead bodies are dangerous. By explaining the proper procedures for handling deceased individuals and emphasising the importance of hygiene, we can dispel these myths and alleviate unnecessary fears. Schools could invite their local funeral director to visit and talk to the children, answering their questions.

Open dialogue plays a vital role in normalising conversations about death and grief. Creating a safe and non-judgmental space for children to share their thoughts, questions, and concerns, we can encourage a culture of openness and understanding. Teachers and school counsellors can facilitate these discussions by using appropriate language, active listening, and empathy.

These conversations also help to challenge the stigma surrounding death and bereavement. The tendency to avoid talking about death, leads to isolation and a lack of support for those who are grieving. Encouraging children to express their emotions and share their experiences, can create a supportive community that validates their feelings and provides comfort during difficult times.

Moreover, this will help to address the misconceptions and stereotypes associated with grief. Children may have preconceived notions that grieving is a sign of weakness, that it should be done privately, or that it has a set timeline. By promoting open discussions, we can challenge these misconceptions and emphasise that grief is a natural and individual process that varies for each person.

Developing empathy and understanding for those who are grieving is an important aspect of learning about death, dying, and bereavement in schools. Promoting compassion and empathy can equip children with the skills and mindset to be supportive and understanding towards their peers who may be experiencing grief.

Empathy is a fundamental human trait that can be nurtured and developed through education. Teaching children about the emotions and challenges associated with grief can help them develop a deeper sense of empathy towards those who are grieving.

One way to encourage empathy is by providing opportunities for children to learn about different experiences of loss and grief. This can be done through storytelling, guest speakers, or discussions about real-life examples. By exposing children to diverse narratives and perspectives, we broaden their understanding of grief and help them recognise the individuality of each person's experience.

In addition to learning about grief, it is important to teach children practical ways to support and be compassionate towards their peers who are grieving. This can include teaching active listening skills, empathy-building exercises, and strategies for offering comfort and support.

Active listening involves giving one's full attention to the person speaking and validating their emotions without judgment. Teaching children to listen actively and empathetically, we empower them to be present for their grieving peers and provide a safe space for expression.

Furthermore, empathy-building exercises can help children understand and relate to the emotions experienced by others. These exercises may involve role-playing, perspective-taking activities, or engaging in reflective discussions. Putting themselves in someone else's shoes can help children develop a deeper appreciation for the complexities of grief and the importance of offering support.

It is also key to emphasise the significance of small acts of kindness and compassion. Simple gestures like offering a listening ear, writing a supportive note, or spending time with a grieving friend can make a significant difference in their healing process.

Teaching children the power of these small acts can empower them to be agents of compassion in their communities.

It is also important to educate children about the impact of their words and actions on others. It can often be the case that bereaved children can become the victims of bullying due to their vulnerabilities while grieving. Equally, they can also become the bully! Children unable to understand their emotions who feel a need to lash out may well do so in the wrong way. Promoting kindness and respect in all interactions can create a safe and inclusive environment where grieving children feel safe, supported and understood.

Incorporating activities that encourage children to open up can be highly beneficial. These activities can include group discussions, storytelling, art projects, or writing exercises. By allowing children to express their thoughts and feelings through different mediums, we can facilitate a deeper understanding of death and grief while promoting empathy and connection among classmates.

Teachers and school administrators can play an important role in cultivating compassion and empathy by providing appropriate training and resources for educators. Professional development sessions can equip teachers with the knowledge and skills to facilitate discussions on death and bereavement effectively. This training should address cultural sensitivity, active listening techniques, and strategies for supporting children who are experiencing grief.

Free school resources and lesson plans can be found on both Child Bereavement UK and Project Eileen's websites.

Respecting Individual Needs

Although many predictable emotions may be displayed, when it comes to supporting children through grief and loss, it is important to recognise and respect the uniqueness of each child's grieving process. Despite the research into how children will respond depending on their developmental stage, each child is still an individual and will deal with it in their own way.

A lot will depend on the character of the child, whether it's the first time they've experienced the death of a loved one and their relationship with that person. It is important to respect individual needs and provide choices and support that align with that child's preferences and beliefs.

Recognising the uniqueness of each child's grieving process: Grief manifests differently in every child. Some may openly express their emotions, while others may internalise them. Some may seek solace in sharing their feelings, while others may prefer to process their grief more privately. It is crucial to acknowledge these individual differences and validate the child's experience without judgment or comparison. By recognising and accepting the uniqueness of each child's grieving process, we create a safe space for them to express themselves authentically. However, it is important to keep checking in with those who want to discuss how they feel and, most definitely, with those who choose not to.

Offering choices and options in how children navigate their grief: Empowering children in their grief journey involves providing them with choices and options, without applying any pressure. Children should be given the opportunity to decide how they want to cope with their loss. This can include offering different activities, such as art therapy, journaling, or physical exercise, and allowing them to choose what resonates with them. Even if their choice is to "carry on as normal", giving children a sense of autonomy, will help them regain control in a situation that can often feel overwhelming and chaotic.

Aiding their emotional literacy: Younger children especially may struggle with the mix of emotions that come with grief. Children may feel guilty if they find themselves playing and having fun. They may not recognise that it is guilt that they are experiencing, or that feeling happy is ok. Finding age-appropriate tools to allow them to discover and deal with what they are feeling would be helpful. Some children may get very angry. It would be useful for them to learn that anger is a secondary emotion and is always triggered by something else. Guide them to recognise what makes them feel angry and then work on that emotion.

Supporting diverse cultural and religious practices related to bereavement: Culture and religion play a significant role in how individuals perceive and cope with death and bereavement. It is essential to respect and support the diverse cultural and religious practices related to grief. This includes understanding the rituals, customs, and beliefs of different communities and offering support that aligns with their specific traditions. Even within a smaller family unit there can be differing beliefs. Acknowledging and embracing cultural and religious diversity demonstrates our commitment to inclusivity and ensures that children feel supported in honouring their heritage while navigating their grief.

Respecting individual needs is a fundamental aspect of empowering the bereaved and helping them find meaning, comfort, and healing in their own way. If you notice a change in behaviour or attitude, even months later, it could be down to how they're dealing with their grief. An angry child isn't always necessarily a naughty child.

A Final Note

The ripple effect of understanding loss is a powerful phenomenon. When we acknowledge and comprehend the depth of grief and its impact on individuals and communities, we become more attuned to the struggles and vulnerabilities of others. Through education and open conversations, we equip ourselves with the knowledge and empathy needed to extend compassion and support to those who are grieving. By understanding the universal nature of loss, we break down barriers of isolation and create a sense of interconnectedness and shared humanity.

Developing compassion is a cornerstone of building kinder and more positive lives. When children and young people are exposed to discussions about grief, death, and bereavement, they learn to empathise with others who are experiencing loss. They develop the capacity to offer support, comfort, and understanding. Compassion becomes a guiding principle in their interactions, allowing them to create a safer and more inclusive environment for their peers. By fostering empathy and compassion in schools, we plant seeds of kindness that have the potential to grow and flourish in our communities.

Schools play a vital role in shaping the future of society. By incorporating discussions on grief and loss into the curriculum, we provide young minds with the tools and knowledge to navigate the complexities of life with kindness and positivity. Through education, children learn about the diverse experiences of grief and gain insight into different cultural and religious practices related to bereavement. This exposure helps to break down stereotypes, challenge misconceptions, and foster a climate of acceptance and understanding.

Having these discussions within schools not only benefits those directly affected by loss but also creates a ripple effect that extends far beyond the classroom. When children learn about grief and loss, they carry that knowledge into their homes, communities, and future interactions. They become advocates for empathy, understanding, and support. They have the potential to inspire their peers, parents, and even teachers to approach life's challenges with compassion and resilience.

Moreover, by addressing grief and loss within the school environment, we send a powerful message to children that their emotional wellbeing matters. We create a culture that values open dialogue, encourages seeking help when needed, and promotes mental health and self-care. By prioritising these discussions, we empower young people to navigate their own grief journeys and develop the skills necessary for lifelong emotional wellbeing.

Notes

Notes

Part 4

Lived Experiences

Lived Experiences

We asked for people's own stories, their views and experience of arranging a funeral and things they'd like others to know that might help. Questions they wish they'd asked when their loved one died and things that they wished they'd known prior to the event.

The response was amazing! From complete strangers on social media, to professional connections, to close friends.

The consistent message was strong; in one way or another, if they can help just one other person going through this process, they are more than happy for their story to be shared.

The stories we received were so powerful that we have edited as little as possible, giving you the raw, real-life emotion of each one.

What we found most interesting is, by sharing with us, many suggested it was a wonderful exercise, incredibly cathartic and, although emotional, they felt better for sharing. Thus, cementing the notion that to talk about, write about or sing about your emotions can only be a good thing!

If I can help one person going through what I went through, it's well-worth it.

I was in my early twenties when it happened and have no relatives of my own. I was inexperienced to say the least and very alone. I knew nothing of death and have spent the subsequent decade reading about death/dying/funerals. I also learned a lot watching the Casketeers (about a Māori funeral home in New Zealand) and After Life - which is a very strong portrayal of grief (it's quite crude at times, but the overall message made up for it to me). I now have a much better understanding of the process, which is bittersweet... But you cannot know what you do not know. You could fill several books with what I did not know, I'm sure.

I did not know that:

- Embalming is not mandatory. That I could have opted to avoid this. That I could have chosen refrigeration. I requested a closed casket and was quite shocked when the staff insisted that we keep it open because of how "good" my husband looked.

- The funeral didn't need to be immediate, that I could have taken more time (they died 2 days apart). Also, that permafrost can prevent burials in some circumstances.

- Buying an expensive casket for a cremation is not necessary.

- About any of the eco-friendlier options such as green burial, aquamation etc.

- That I had options - that I could have chosen to move him to a different funeral home or bought a coffin elsewhere and had it brought in.

- That witnessed cremation is possible - I think this would have provided far more closure for me.

- Cremation stones/diamonds were possible or that cremation jewellery was an option.

- About infant bereavement photography or cuddle cots - two things I would have used given the chance.

- About weighted teddy bears symbolising neonatal losses.

- Cemeteries can be incredibly restrictive about types of monuments, what you can plant (trees) and what you can leave or not at the grave (pinwheels, toys).

I was unprepared for:

- The cost - it was astronomical.

- For the amount/volume of my husband's ashes I received. There was twice-as much as would fit into the urn I had chosen. I scattered half his ashes and kept the other half.

- I was extremely unprepared for the colour & consistency of his ashes. I'm not 100% sure something didn't go wrong with the cremulator - but there were small pieces of discernible bone. There was also a metal bracket that fell to the ground and made a loud noise bouncing off a rock as well as the metal cremation tab. A friend of mine climbed down the forest ledge to retrieve the tab among the scattered ashes because we didn't know what it was, and he was afraid it was important and/or of sentimental value - it just had the cemetery crest and an identification number.

- The number of in-person appointments it would take to close accounts and how obtuse staff can be "he's going to have to co-sign" ... sigh.

- The amount of funeral director's certificates of death I would require.

One thing the funeral director did help me with was to avoid having the funeral around a mealtime so that I only had to pay for coffee, tea & treats instead of a full lunch of sandwiches etc.

At the end of the day, funerals are for the living. You're asked to make terrible & impossible decisions at the worst moment of your life. Give yourself some grace. Don't worry about what others are going to think and do what feels less worse (nothing will feel good). Want a colour instead of black? - use it. Want a song? - play it. Balloons? - send them into the sky. Want to speak? - go ahead. You might cry, you might not. That doesn't mean you love them any less if you don't or can't. Let people help you but do the things you need to do to survive this time and express your grief. Repressing it will only make it worse.

Funerals (& grief) bring out the best in some, and the absolute worst in others. People don't know what to say, and often in trying to relate to you, compare completely incomparable things to your grief. They mean well, which makes you feel guilty at the fact you just want to scream at them to shut up - that your baby dying is nothing like their loss of their childhood dog... and yes, I know I'm young, but I want my husband, not some new random guy...

Grief

- Support for your grief lasts about a month (6 months for close friends/family), and then they forget & move on (and want & expect you to do the same). Grievers know, there is no timeline. The best thing you can do is to find one of us. It's ok to be sad. Seek help, but not all providers are grief-informed - do your research. As Megan Devine says: Some things cannot be fixed, they can only be carried.

- Grief comes in waves - there is not always rhyme or reason. Everyone grieves differently, what helps others might not help you.

- You will lose some friends, but you will find others.

- Nothing & no-one is perfect - it's ok to acknowledge the good & the bad about your person. That's what makes them real. It's ok to be angry with them. It's ok to love and miss them. It's ok & normal to grieve the loss of the life you would have had together.

Name: Wendy

Lost: Dad

I don't mind talking about my dad - even the tough stuff - because it's so important that people know what to expect, to make it that little less scary.

I was very lucky that I used the funeral directors in the village where my parents live - they have done most of the relatives' funerals and they are very lovely people. I do remember thinking 'I don't actually know what happens to dad's body now' - I imagined the funeral directors turning up and collecting him from the hospital ward. I realise now that clearly wasn't going to happen! I do remember the funeral director ringing me and saying 'I'm just ringing to let you know that we've got your dad' - but it was about four days after he'd died I think - and I didn't like the idea of him having been in the mortuary at the hospital for that time. I was very relieved to think that he was in their 'custody'.

I think if I was to give one word of advice to people who are facing the funeral arrangements - it's that they should not be frightened to just take stock and take time to work out what they really want. I'm not suggesting that funeral directors rush families into arrangements - but I think people feel obliged to get the funeral organised asap - and I'm not sure why. My dad was buried in the cemetery in the village - it's next to the community centre - and we had a celebrant rather than a church service. It did raise the issue of where we were going to hold the service - so I asked the funeral director if we could hold it in the community centre and then have the wake there, after the burial. They'd never done it before but he asked the village council and they agreed and that's what we did. And I'm so glad I asked the question - and that's what people should be encouraged to do.

There were more questions than I expected - like what colour we wanted the coffin lined in (magnolia of course - dad's favourite colour!) - or whether we wanted dad to be wearing any particular clothes (dressing gown - his favourite item of clothing when he was ill).

On a purely practical level - I wish my dad hadn't had premium bonds. Every other asset my parents owned, were in their joint names, so passed over to mum on just sight of the death certificate (bank accounts, title to the house etc). But because dad had premium bonds (which can only be held in a single name) - I had to apply for a grant of probate in order to cash them in - which was a massive faff - for not a lot of money! But that's more of a pre-death bit of advice!

I often hear the direct cremation adverts talking about the 'stress' of organising a funeral, and 'no one wants a funeral' - and it makes my blood boil - because that just isn't true for everyone. I, and I know my mum, got such a lot of comfort from seeing the people who turned up the funeral - dad's old work colleagues, next door neighbours, lifelong friends etc. I wouldn't have swapped it for the world and I still get comfort from it now when I think about it.

John, in his role as Funeral Director

I arranged a funeral for a young man who had died by suicide. There was no inkling at all that this may be a possibility by the family and they were in complete shock.

When they came into our offices to arrange the funeral, I could see how distraught and desperate the mother was. I asked if she had any questions or concerns before we went through any details. The mother responded with how she wanted to come and see her son straight away - she was desperate to see him. When discussing arrangements, I asked if she would like to assist in dressing and preparing her son. She was overwhelmed and relieved to be able to be part of this. She was obviously very nervous but I recognised how important it was for her.

A few days later when she came to help prepare her son, I wanted to show her the mortuary space prior to presenting her son to get her used to the space. Once we'd shown her, we took her back to our office and had a cup of tea. During this time we placed candles in the mortuary space and put on their favourite band, Queen, very quietly in the background to take away the silence. When I returned her to the mortuary space, with my colleague Darren's support she placed on the socks of her son. I remember her saying how she was the first person to put on his socks and how important it was to be the last. This was a beautiful example of a connection point.

The night before the funeral, the family had a glass of champagne in the chapel. I felt very privileged to be involved in this. Prior to them leaving our facility, I explained that when they go tonight, I will be placing the lid on the coffin and asked if they wanted to assist me. I always feel funeral directors have a huge honour to be the last person to see a deceased person - therefore why shouldn't the family be the last? They helped close the coffin being the last to see him. They each took a screw and helped in securing the coffin. What I witnessed was beautiful, stunning and I stand by the belief as a family they will now move forward in a different way.

Name: Helen

Lost: Mum and preparing for Dad's death

In memory of Josephine MacRae

I'd be delighted to share my experiences. My dad has actually been receiving palliative care since December, so as an adult I am also learning the process of 'what to do, practically, when someone dies.' After listening to one of John's podcasts, I phoned the funeral director. I had so many over-whelming questions in my head and planning dad's funeral and what will come afterwards felt like a huge mountain ahead. So when I listened to the podcast it gave me a big shift in my thinking, knowing the funeral directors were there to help - at all stages. I think more people could benefit from that knowledge.

When I phoned I was met with the most wonderfully caring and supportive lady on the end of the phone. I asked my main question, 'What do I actually do when he dies? Do I phone 999?!' At that point I burst into tears because the reality hit (and I felt a bit silly for not knowing!), but she was so patient and told me to take me time. She spoke through the step by step of calling the GP when we were ready to gain the 'certification of death,' then when we were ready to phone them, any time of day or night and they would collect dad - again, whenever it suited us. She also explained they had a leaflet that I was welcome to pick up and that I was welcome to visit for a coffee and a chat anytime I was passing. Knowing this support was available has been wonderful - I haven't needed it, but knowing it's there means the world.

I am fortunate to have done so much training with Child Bereavement UK, so I have been able to talk openly with my two sons about grandpa's health and have involved them in thinking about the funeral and any part they would like to play. But I think this is key information for families - involving the children so they feel part of the process. My youngest really struggles with the time I have to take out of every day to care for my dad and often moans that I'm too busy - so also making sure I intentionally spent quality 1:1 time with him every week has been really helpful for him - and my mum guilt!

I also reached out to a close friend to ask in advance that my church family support us with meals for a few days after dad dies - so that my sons are provided for and my husband is supported - knowing I'll be busy! It took a lot of courage asking for help - but I didn't think I'd have the capacity or courage to ask in the midst of the grief. It's good for people to know that taking a meal over, even if they don't know what to say, is a huge help.

In terms of my mum's funeral, I don't remember being involved at all, but I tried to be out of the home as much as possible. I remember feeling relieved when she'd died because it was so hard caring for her and seeing her so poorly. Selfishly, I also wanted someone to take care of me for a change - life for 18 months had been all about her. (This is my teenage brain thinking!!) So I then looked forward to the funeral because people would be there for me, I loved receiving all the cards and hugs and attention. After the funeral when all that stopped, was the most grim months of my life and I considered death by suicide several times. Dad was awful and I had so much responsibility on my shoulders. I remember being asked once if I wanted to speak to someone, but never did and regret it now.

So, what would I want people to know from my experience? Letting me know my 'selfish' feelings were ok, I suffered from the guilt of that reaction for many years. I'd have loved someone to persevere with offering me help over the months and years that followed so that I knew I could reach out - someone said to me a year after she died, "Haven't you got over this yet?" So I felt I wasn't normal and tried to cover up my grief for YEARS.

The only other thing that jumps out at me regarding mum's funeral is that it was celebration of her life. People were asked to wear bright colours and to rejoice at her life. I hated that because I felt I wasn't allowed to be sad or to grieve. People were putting on a brave face all around me and I wished someone had burst into tears, so I could do the same. We will be wearing black for my dad's funeral - as are his wishes - with his tartan as a sash for the ladies and kilts or ties for the lads - but being able to mourn is something we need to be able to do - amongst the celebration and recognition of his life.

On a practical note, my dad has an insurance policy that will pay out to help cover his funeral costs - I didn't realise just how expensive they were until we started this process. So for people to think ahead to provide this for their families or to be sign-posted to where they can get financial support if they can't afford the costs, would be helpful.

Crikey, that has been a healing process! Thank you for giving me a voice for my grief.

Name: Jon

Lost: Son

I lost my teenage son Max in May 2021.

Max's funeral

It was at the end of May 2021, there were still some restrictions on gatherings but we were allowed around 90 for the service as the crematorium had 2 rooms, 1 with a large screen. For the wake/gathering afterwards I think it was restricted to 35/40. We took the decision that the wake was for immediate family and Max's friends as places were limited. Other family members that had travelled to attend the service weren't invited. Sure a few were put out by this, but Max's friends & teachers were our priority.

It all feels quite distant now, after almost three years, but I do remember the kindness and assistance of Julien our funeral director. The cost was kept low, as they had some funds for under 16s. I remember the language and tone was always kind, for example "Max is with us now" and not "we've collected Max's body". They put us in touch with a wonderful celebrant for the service.

Grief in general

So much has 'worked' for us over the last three years. A few things to expect because they seem to happen to everyone, people will come and go in your lives, we have wonderful new supportive friends, but some people haven't stepped up and have fallen away. We were lucky enough to have six months paid bereavement leave, we signed up to Borrow My Doggy and started walking a lovely dog called Hugo. We ended up after much consideration rehoming a dog of our own, Monty, in February 22. Other advice, find support in your own time, but be open to it. I started therapy very early, about 5 weeks after Max died by suicide, as I know that the trauma of finding him on that day required professional help, I also didn't want to burden others with something that horrible.

I attended the home of a gentleman whose wife had died, they have three children. When I arrived at the family home in the early hours on a weekend, the house was full of people - all extended family who were there to show their love and support. It was important I gathered the immediate family to explain the next steps. This was an opportunity to create calmness and control which cannot be emphasised enough during a time of loss.

I explained to the children that we would be leaving their home with their mum and making our way to our funeral home. Despite their mum leaving the home at that time, it was vital they knew that their mum remained theirs. She did not become mine or the funeral homes. I explained that during the next week or so I would talk through lots of ideas to prove this and empower them to make this difficult time a special time.

Before the date of the funeral, we took mum's fingerprints together, deciding to eventually take all of the family's fingerprints. All sets of fingerprints are now on the headstone of mum. This is such a great example of creating true connection. The family went on to appear on BBC breakfast with me during the time of the parliament petition. The husband of the lady who had died showed great bravery in his communication and how he allowed the children to be involved. The family were the true example of empowerment which resulted in them moving forward with their grief in a more positive way.

Practical Advice & Resources

Child Bereavement UK and Project Eileen, along with similar organisations, offer a range of resources and services that complement the strategies covered in this book and provide specialised support.

Child Bereavement UK, renowned for their expertise in supporting children and families through the grieving process, offer a wide range of services and resources. Their helpline provides a confidential space for individuals to seek guidance and support from trained professionals who understand the complexities of child bereavement. They also offer face-to-face support sessions, and groups for children, young people and parents designed to address the unique needs of bereaved children and families.

www.childbereavementuk.org

Helpline: 0800 02 888 40

Project Eileen, another notable charity, focuses on providing grief support and education within school settings. Their comprehensive lesson plans for schools cover topics such as death, dying, and bereavement, ensuring that children have access to age-appropriate information and support. By integrating these lesson plans into the National Curriculum, Project Eileen has successfully raised awareness about the importance of discussing death and bereavement in schools.

www.projecteileen.co.uk

The Good Grief Trust exists to help all those affected by grief in the UK. Their vision is to help those bereaved from day one, acknowledge their grief and provide reassurance, a virtual hand of friendship and ongoing support. Run by the bereaved, for the bereaved, they aim to encourage talking about grief in a more honest, straightforward way, help to make the pain a little more bearable for those at the early stages and offer inspiration and hope to the bereaved further along their own grief 'journey'.

thegoodgrieftrust.org

The work of organisations like Child Bereavement UK, Project Eileen and The Good Grief Trust, highlights the collective effort to ensure that children and families receive the necessary support during times of grief. By providing accessible resources, guidance, and professional assistance, these charities play a vital role in creating a compassionate and understanding society.

It is essential to recognise that every individual's grief journey is unique. What works for one person may not work for another. Therefore, the tools and resources provided by organisations like Child Bereavement UK and Project Eileen serve as valuable options for individuals to explore and determine what best suits their needs.

The sponsors who made this happen:

www.westerleighgroup.co.uk

"Westerleigh Group is the leading developer and operator of crematoria and cemeteries in the UK caring for approximately 71,000 funerals a year.

We have proven expertise and have established a reputation for creating beautifully landscaped, high quality and peaceful facilities with service to the bereaved at their heart."

www.muchloved.com

"MuchLoved is the UK's leading tribute website service, hosting sites for over 300,000 users which have raised over £150 million for good causes. In 2024 we changed to become a social enterprise; an investment in our future to ensure our long-term sustainability.

The MuchLoved tribute service is quick and simple to set up and use. It provides you with the very best way to record and share your memories and stories. You can add pictures, music and video, as well as light virtual candles to help you create a truly special and unique tribute site."

www.flexmort.com

"Flexmort's mortuary storage and cooling systems have revolutionised mobile body storage allowing the deceased to be cooled with dignity and without the need for large traditional mortuary refrigerators.

Our mobile body cooling solutions include cooling a single deceased person on a bed or trolley with a cooling blanket, cooling a deceased neonatal in a cooling cot as well as providing large mobile mass fatality mortuary systems."

Acknowledgements

The most exciting achievements in life are the ones you complete as a team, this book has been a team effort and author Clare Shaw has been the driving force in its delivery. Her own experiences of loss, combined with the incredible books she has written to support child loss is the key to this books success.

I would also like thank the sponsors of this book: Flexmort, Westerleigh Group and Much Loved.

Their support in my mission has been a constant and with their shared views on why we should want to improve the experience of death, dying and bereavement in society. I am grateful beyond words for their support.

Chris and Katie, onwards together - always.

Finally, Adele, Jack, Luke & Elodie, thank you for allowing me to go on this journey, I believe and hope your support you have given me will eventually help others when they go through the most difficult challenges of their lives.

Maria Adams, what a mum, you have been the fuel throughout all my accomplishments.

John Adams

To find out more about both authors, John and Clare, please visit their websites:

John - perryandphillipsfunerals.com

Clare - cskidsbooks.com

Podcast - achangingindustry.com

Notes

Notes

Other titles from Clare Shaw

Love Will Never Die

Following the death of a loved one, it is vital that children have the opportunity to grieve. Using direct but child-friendly language, this book addresses the mixed emotions felt by a child during that process. It offers support and understanding alongside areas where the child can express themselves through writing and drawing.

It also houses a packet of tissues and an envelope to keep 'special things'.

A Mind Full of Grief

When someone you love dies, what happens next?

As a teenager or young adult, this can be such a confusing time. So many emotions you may not have felt before.

So much confusion.

This book will help you through. Filled with practical and honest information but without overloading.

Covering everything from grief and the funeral to the future in the most straightforward way.

At Times I Get These Feelings

Children can often find it difficult to identify with an emotion. It isn't always easy for them to articulate what they are feeling.

This brilliantly written book covers twelve main emotions and is packed full of tips and activities to help children with their emotional literacy. From happy to embarrassed, to jealous or angry, it touches on each emotion offering talking points around some of the trickier feelings.

Bold images and colours to match the emotion make it bright and engaging for the child. With an interactive element, the child can write and draw their own thoughts and feelings too.

This book would be a valuable addition to any child's library.

cskidsbooks.com